DEER

HOUR

KHATY XIONG

DEER

HOUR

KHATY XIONG

NEW MICHIGAN PRESS
TUCSON, ARIZONA

NEW MICHIGAN PRESS
DEPT OF ENGLISH, P. O. BOX 210067
UNIVERSITY OF ARIZONA
TUCSON, AZ 85721-0067

<http://newmichiganpress.com/nmp>

Orders and queries to nmp@thediagram.com.

Copyright © 2014 by Khaty Xiong.
All rights reserved.

ISBN 978-1-934832-46-2. FIRST PRINTING.

Printed in the United States of America.

Design by Ander Monson.

Cover image © Khaty Xiong

CONTENTS

—we write to come   1
In the winter   2
More formally—   3
In this valley we begin   4
With one phase it goes…   5
to be calm / claim with   6
In a dumb bind such as   7
Yet what can be more curious   8
O, do not feed them…   9
there / for sin   10
An overlord rises…   11
I awoke to   12
We grow tired of hearing…   13
Your face keeps coming back…   14
(Spring, sometime ago)   15
of story, exiled against…   16
The sun as we do goes   17
([an]other revelation)   18
We'll keep entering the spaces…   19
Praise the storm, its mechanism   20
—to step back & know a master   21
—in a civilized dream   22

There is snow here, wind   23
Would you have me   24
Here at the turn   25
Sweet again—   26

Acknowledgments   29

—we write to come
to what so many
    stare in wonder—
to make a plot—
to rotate the storm—

something to lift the air
process the darkness
    we have become—

In the winter
you begin to understand
these places are not for you

    your own body to help you
    to collapse inside quietly—
    we don't know anything.

Alone is each making—
of years naming remains

this fragment replicates
    the weight of body parts
        with each to show us
        we are
        to fall now

        to keep this going—

From the looking images
a bog is a terrifying place to be a fly—

you tell me what that means

More formally—

you watch for wolves in the dark
bones you claim impossibly full—

>From the dead comes the order—
a different taste for blood

—there's a place of becoming
other than whole body, an ear—

Migrating across the wetlands
Red-winged Blackbirds

your pines praying loudly, crouched
on a grave, most wild—

In this valley we begin
    the gesture of clashing—

ghosts to tend our treasons

For every deer hour
    you sound
from the north—

untouch my calm…
    In this weather

we hide
    in its plainness—

vanishing—white—
& burning—

With one phase it goes for her young

& on the verge of
   habitat

an herbal hunger
with the exception of

      your 18 doves amassed
      & singing

      —tender when fed
      naked below ebony waist

>   to be calm / claim with
>   evidence
>   our limits
>   patrolled / in its usual
>   rhythms
>   a man
>   clutching the body
>   that would
>   dispel

In a dumb bind such as
this you offer the raw virgin
for a better season—

    Two drops in
        a boy in the form
    of cabbage his eyes
    in the image of earth

You sabotage
    all relations
before the air clears
you allow
    the first word
to pass

Yet what can be more curious
we are given the same subject
a new curriculum for theory—

our divide in the epicenter of
    man-made revolution
the pace of the city too fast
    for memory—

We could not have prepared
an army to love us—

O, do not feed them—of hands
   to tear down—to hatch
      a primitive floating of the past—

This region sprouts a human march—
   bound in sore action
—unable to reconcile
   the wild & the not-wild

                Yet a storm giveth too—

    for unlike anything the soil is sacred—
    animals mystical through songbirds—
    meat-eaters resembling tragic remains—

        Call it—a system to keep—
        a den or refuge for light
        made by ancient mouths—

    In a dream we descend nowhere fast
    reaching places we've never been—

    there
        for sin
we eat
        store notes
            of the
            center of the
        know
& it could
        temple—
            relight
        the mantra of
which is where
        & another without
            rising from
        a closure for
this nostalgic
        hunger

An overlord rises from the harbor
   this morning

medicine so thick I lean
into the ground / in order

to howl through the colony

        & how do you receive
        my calls—

my thumb alone controlled
by nine separate muscles
the larynx by animal will

I awoke to
the sounds of Dark-
    eyed Juncos—
their fragile winter
in the form of
        my childhood

Resigned to
tribal lands, the hum of
    nothing—the weary
birds come with
a good blizzard

    Pine Siskins rest-
    less & ready with
        the torched refrain
    in a language whose
    origins are bound
        to no end

    We grow tired of hearing each other
& cleave to this landscape—

In dreams, it is customary to catch fire—
    to see the occasional orchid, rarely a vine—
to become particles entering the ionosphere…

    Caught in my throat—
a bird that opened itself—claws against
    howling winds, the thick living—

On the Maalah cliffs, a desert rose anchors itself

Your face keeps coming back—small, thick-skinned—
 a swelling hole unseen… Here, out of touch—

the resemblance is carved away to make room for
 this killing field crowned by a kestrel, the flat line

to envelop us. We took refuge to understand
 the (tomentose) blade, (arachnoid) lobe—

the above & below. Between trappings we paced
 ourselves navigating the grief—

a ghostly cackle or whine, your stomach wind-savaged—
 clear & pulsing. I waited for the smoky sway of

your wrist or forearm, wild shapes, the rise of the edible sun—

(Spring, sometime ago)

A saint once stopped to pray
for a language buried inside this map

    —out of the forest came a song
    for the hunt, a door to
amnesia / pastures like
a hairy caterpillar, childhood
    writing from the front lines—

of story, exiled against / pushed & left panting

    the wandered schizophrenic
    reborn as

    —worlds of cannot be
            cut off
        deeply

The sun as we do goes
missing—our machinery
of that unexceptional star

> When we catch prey / it is
> the all-knowing / anatomical
>   plan just as

a cat drawing to its mouth
the prey in this / common
    hour

([an]other revelation)

The hand was formed to hold a weapon—
to drive away mystery from the natural world

The human voice often returns "like this" you say, turning
from the soil—becoming full of form: unpalatable

For instance, one has to translate through the eyes—
see how a fist spreads in this fine holding

Still, an ear is something more primal, possessed of
a natural frontier: there is no other—

                Today, the air grows dense. I press here
                & there to recite, to document again & again

We'll keep entering the spaces of our ancestors
—wade through the marshes of stories
—eat in the process so we do not starve…

The world as we know it builds for the comfort of
    ghosts—slashing portals—

In the sere palm of day—
    worms are one with the dark

Praise the storm, its mechanism

a ptarmigan fluttering out of snow

a teachable alchemy made loose

calibrating in the fourth state of matter

red cedars whose secrets keep us logging

the song of a Horned Lark mapped & charged

—to step back & know a master
of its climate—silica—one
    bite at a time…

Direct my thunder-
head
    smoke & salt it
bring over
    your jars

—in a civilized dream

we mistake the aurora
for sunrise

riddles becoming other than
air-conditioned quarters

proof the hand can dig
remove tumors & pull
a rabbit out of a hat

There is snow here, wind
from the north—

We sever our ties & the ground is
    a mere membrane
between sky & more sky—

a chicken's neck is the same
& God crows on the other side

Would you have me
doubt the arm
   its wrist / a floating
cluster / the human
   variations of
molecular under-
standing / the human
   brain in misfire digits
talk against the white
armored hillsides
   —could I do it
in a parade
   & do it well

Here at the turn
of floral breath—
    a sleep demon's dirge—

Swathed in premature rain—
city fawns in the love song
    of a bluebird—

Sweet again—
between truth & how fire is made
   it is your birthday—
     the water, grass & weeds
   give desert a name—

In the distant field
   animals breathe
each other's dust

   replace, hang & remove

ACKNOWLEDGMENTS

Thank you to *MiPOesias* in which poems from this manuscript—"In the winter," "More formally," and "An overlord rises…"—originally appeared in its 2014 summer issue.

Thank you to the editors of *DIAGRAM* for selecting my manuscript for publication, to Ander for making this book possible, and heartfelt thanks to the individuals who inspired these poems.

KHATY XIONG is a second-generation Hmong-American from Fresno, CA. She received her MFA in Poetry from the University of Montana, where she was also the 2013 recipient of the Merriam-Frontier Award for her first poetry chapbook *Elegies*. Her first book of poetry *Poor Anima* is forthcoming from Apogee Press. Her work has appeared in *How Do I Begin?: A Hmong American Literary Anthology, Kartika Review, Lantern Review, Alice Blue Review, The Poet's Billow, Indefinite Space, Birdfeast, MiPOesias, New Nowhere*, and *inter|rupture*. Currently, she resides in Dublin, OH.

COLOPHON

Text is set in a digital version of Jenson, designed by Robert Slimbach in 1996, and based on the work of punchcutter, printer, and publisher Nicolas Jenson. The titles are in Futura.

NEW MICHIGAN PRESS, based in Tucson, Arizona, prints poetry and prose chapbooks, especially work that transcends traditional genre. Together with DIAGRAM, NMP sponsors a yearly chapbook competition.

DIAGRAM, a journal of text, art, and schematic, is published bimonthly at THEDIAGRAM.COM. Periodic print anthologies are available from the New Michigan Press at NEWMICHIGANPRESS.COM/NMP.

www.ingramcontent.com/pod-product-compliance
Lightning Source LLC
Chambersburg PA
CBHW031507040426
42444CB00007B/1240